Getting To Know...

Nature's Children

DEER

Laima Dingwall

Grolier

Facts in Brief

Classification of the White-tailed Deer

    Class: *Mammalia* (mammals)
    Order: *Artiodactyla* (cloven-hoofed mammal)
    Family: *Cervidae* (deer family)
    Genus: *Odocoileus*
    Species: *Odocoileus virginianus* (Virginia Deer)

World distribution. Exclusive to North America. Other members of the deer family are found in North, South, and Central America, Europe, and Asia.

Habitat. Woods and brushlands.

Distinctive physical characteristics. Longer tail than other deer; underside of tail pure white.

Habits. Relatively solitary but may gather in groups in winter (called *yarding*); snorts when alarmed and may thump the ground with its front hoofs; in full flight flips up its tail, showing white fur underneath.

Diet. Leaves, grass, twigs, buds, fruits, berries, mushrooms.

Edited by: Elizabeth Grace Zuraw
Design/Photo Editor: Nancy Norton
Photo Rights: Ivy Images

ISBN: 0-7172-8489-1

Have you ever wondered . . .

What's the first thing that comes to mind when you hear the word *deer?*

Perhaps you think of the magnificent antlers or the swift grace of deer you have seen. Maybe you think of deer-crossing signs on highways warning drivers that a deer might suddenly burst out of the woods into the path of their cars.

Chances are, however, that you probably think of Bambi. Although Walt Disney made the animated movie "Bambi" many years ago, his little fawn is still one of the first things most people think of when deer come to mind.

It's easy to understand why. With his big eyes, sweet face, and graceful way of moving, Bambi was truly one of the most beautiful animals in the forest.

This is just as true of real deer. And there's a good chance that you have seen a real deer, either in a zoo or in the woods. After all, there are close to 20 million deer in North America.

Sleek, graceful, timid, and alert, deer are common to most of North America.

Meet the Relatives

If the White-tailed Deer held a family reunion for its North American relatives, who would come? Its close cousin, the Mule Deer, of course, and its other cousins, the elk, moose, and caribou.

All these members of the deer family have a number of traits in common. For instance, none has any top front teeth, they all have split hoofs for feet, and they all chew the *cud,* food swallowed and brought up later for chewing.

Of course, some or even all of these things are true of other animals as well. But members of the deer family have one more feature in common: each year the males grow and shed a pair of *antlers,* hard, bony growths on their heads. This is what makes deer different from all other hoofed animals.

As this elk shows, one feature common to al members of the deer family is antlers—but only males grow them.

6

White-tailed Deer Country

Of the approximately 20 million deer in North America, about 14 million are White-tailed Deer. They are found across the central and southern parts of the continent, except in the high mountains and deserts of the far West.

Look for White-tailed Deer near clearings around forests, on the edges of swamps and glades, near the banks of streams and ponds, and close to farmland. These are the places where the deer can find the plants, shrubs, and small trees they need for food and protection.

Deer Up Close

There are about 30 varieties of White-tailed Deer in North America. Most are quite similar in appearance and behavior. In fact, it's often difficult to tell them apart—except, in some cases, by their size.

Opposite page: Deer can often be seen near water and in clearings along roads and highways.

Where deer are found in North America

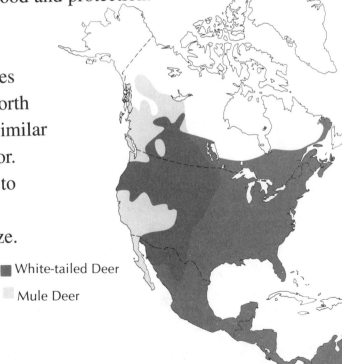

■ White-tailed Deer

▨ Mule Deer

Deer that live in cold climates tend to be larger than those living in warm areas. They need a large body, which doesn't lose heat as fast as a small one. In northern regions, a full-grown male deer, called a *buck,* stands about 38 inches tall (just under 1 meter) from its hoofs to the top of its shoulders. A buck weighs more than most adult men. The female, called a *doe,* is slightly smaller. In southern areas such as Florida, deer weigh only about half as much as their northern cousins.

In summer a deer has a short, reddish-brown coat make of stiff, wiry hairs. Deer start getting ready for winter in late August by replacing their summer coat with a thick, gray-blue winter one. The hairs in this coat are long and hollow. They trap the air warmed by the deer's body heat and help keep the animal cozy even in the coldest weather. In winter, the deer also grows an undercoat of downy hairs for extra warmth.

Deer tend to be larger the farther north they live. And a deer can increase its size if it has a plentiful supply of good food.

The Mule Deer

After the White-tailed Deer, the most common deer in North America is the Mule Deer. It lives in the open forests, brush, and parklands of western North America.

You can tell a Mule Deer from a White-tailed Deer in four ways.

First, the antlers of a Mule Deer buck branch from the stem in pairs rather than singly. The second thing you notice is that the Mule Deer's ears are huge. In fact, this deer got its name because its ears reminded people of a mule's big ears. The Mule Deer also has an unusual way of moving. When it bounds, it keeps its legs very stiff, and its four feet land on the ground at the same time. Last, but not least, the Mule Deer has a short black-tipped tail. And unlike the White-tailed Deer, when the Mule Deer is frightened, its tail doesn't flip up and wave like a flag.

Antlers

White-tailed Deer

Mule Deer

Can you guess what kind of deer these are? Hint: look at those oversized ears. Do they remind you of a mule's big ears?

12

A Rack of Antlers

Imagine carrying this load on your head: a rack of antlers as wide as your outstretched arms and as heavy as a bag of potatoes! That's the size of antlers on the average full-grown buck.

Only male deer grow antlers, and they grow a new set every year. They use them mainly to fight other bucks for mates or to ward off wolves.

Antlers start to develop in spring. While they are growing, they're covered with a thick, soft skin called *velvet.* This skin contains the blood vessels that nourish the antlers as they grow.

By late summer, the antlers are full-grown, and the velvety skin starts to dry up and peel off. This can make a buck look awfully messy! But not for long. The buck helps get rid of the shaggy strips of hanging velvet by rubbing his antlers against trees.

A buck loses his antlers one at a time in early winter. They break off next to the deer's head. A buck may have red sores in those spots for a few days, but these soon heal.

Opposite page:
Velvet *is a fitting name for the special layer of skin on a buck's growing antlers. The skin is soft, fuzzy, and thick, just like velvet cloth.*

Once the antlers are on the ground, little creatures such as mice and chipmunks are quick to come and nibble at them. Antlers are full of calcium and other minerals that are good for these little animals.

Big, Bigger, Biggest

A buck will probably grow his first pair of antlers during the second summer of his life. Often these will just be smooth, straight spikes, about 5 inches (12-13 centimeters) long. Where good food is plentiful, however, these first antlers may develop several branches, or *points.* By the time a buck is four or five years old, his antlers will usually have about eight points, though many more can grow.

Some people think you can tell the age of a buck by the size of his antlers or by the number of points on them. This is not true. Once a buck is full-grown—at age four or so—the size of his antlers depends mainly on how healthy he is. A buck that is getting plenty of good food to eat will usually grow the biggest set of antlers.

Opposite page:
Four points on each antler make this an eight-point buck. Bucks use their antlers to fight for mates. But the fights seldom are really serious—more like a shoving match.

Seeing, Smelling, and Hearing

If you were to put on your brightest red sweater and could stand perfectly still in front of a deer, it might not even notice you. That's because deer are color-blind. Those big, soft brown eyes see the world in shades of gray— a little like watching a black and white TV. To the deer, you'd be just another grayish pattern in the forest. But move—even just blink an eye—and a deer, with its excellent ability to spot movement, will see you.

And if you ever think of trying to sneak up on a deer from behind, don't bother—unless the wind is blowing in the right direction, toward you and away from the deer. A deer has a very keen sense of smell. If the wind is carrying your scent its way, the deer will pick it up and be gone long before you can get near.

Deer are timid creatures. They can't defend themselves very effectively if attacked, so they take off at the first sign of danger.

This bounding deer offers positive identification. It has antlers—so it's a male. And a white underside is revealed when its tail is raised—so it's a White-tailed Deer.

Even if the deer doesn't smell you, it will probably hear you. Deer have a very sharp sense of hearing, too. When a deer cocks its pointy ears, it can hear sounds long before you can. The first strange sound might not send it fleeing, but a second or a third will surely send it bounding away.

Deer on the Move

Watch a deer bound and you would swear it has springs in its legs. First, its two front legs touch the ground at the same time, then its two back legs touch down. It takes a deer three short bounds and then one big l-e-a-p to cover a distance about the length of a van.

A deer can run as fast as a horse over short distances. Even a pile of rocks or a fence will not slow it down. It can clear obstacles 10 feet (3 meters) high—about the height of two medium-sized cars stacked on top of each other!

Deer Tracks

Buck

Doe

Fawn

If there's a pond in a deer's path, that's no problem either. Instead of changing direction, the deer is just as likely to leap right into the water and swim across. Deer are very good swimmers. During the late spring and summer, deer often wade neck-deep in nearby lakes to get away from pesky black flies and mosquitoes.

A deer's hoofs give it a good grip when it's running on hard ground. But on ice the hoofs slip and slide. Nor are the sharp hoofs good for running on top of deep snow. The hoofs sink down easily and prevent the deer from moving quickly. Getting around in winter can be a problem for deer.

It's easy to see why deep snow is a serious problem for deer.

The Deer's Home

It may seem surprising, since deer are such good runners, but these animals are real homebodies. They don't travel far from their territory unless there is a shortage of food. A deer's *territory*—the area it considers "home"—is often no bigger than about 1 square mile (under 2 square kilometers). Up to 30 or more adult deer can share a territory this size in an area where there is plenty of food.

Within its territory, a deer does not build a nest or a den like some other animals. Instead, it beds down in any place that looks safe and comfortable. That is often on dry, smooth ground surrounded by trees. In winter, a deer often picks a sheltered spot under low-hanging evergreen branches. But wherever it settles down, a deer makes sure that it is not too far from a feeding spot.

Deer tend to stay within a fairly small territory. But when food is scarce, they sometimes have to travel many miles to find good winter feeding grounds.

Dinnertime

Don't ask a deer to smile. That's because it doesn't have any top front teeth! Instead it has a tough pad that it uses for tearing plants and twigs. But to chew its food, a deer has 32 teeth in the rest of its mouth.

What do deer eat? That depends on the season. In spring and summer, grass and other plants top the list, followed closely by tender twigs, buds, and leaves from shrubs and trees. In fall, deer add acorns and mushrooms to their diet. Apples are favorite treats, and deer will even rear up on their hind legs to reach into a tree to pull down one of these sweet, juicy fruits.

Deer eat a lot—about 15 pounds (7 kilograms) of food on a good summer day.

Eat Now, Chew Later

Deer usually feed in the early morning and again in the evening. They keep moving around as they eat and don't waste much time chewing. That's because deer, like cows, are cud chewers.

Spring at last! Velvet-covered antlers are growing, and a rich supply of juicy twigs and buds will soon fatten up this buck.

You can tell a branch that's been chewed by a deer by its ragged end. Since deer have no top front teeth, they tear food rather than cut it cleanly.

Being a cud chewer means that a deer can swallow first and chew later. A special part of a deer's stomach collects the unchewed food. Then the deer looks for a resting spot that is safe from enemies and out of the hot sun or cold winter winds. There the deer brings the stored food, the cud, back to its mouth and chews it in peace. Deer usually lie down to chew—maybe because it's such tiring work. After all, they give each piece of lemon-sized cud about 40 good chews!

Winter Feeding

Unlike squirrels and some other animals, deer do not store food for winter. Instead, they eat what they can find. If there is only a little snow on the ground, deer uncover moss, leaves, and even acorns with their hoofs. If the snow is deep and covers up food of this kind, they eat branches and twigs from trees such as birch, willow, and evergreens. And if a deer cannot find enough twigs or branches, it strips bark from trees and eats that.

Deer usually eat facing into the wind so that they have a better chance of catching any strange scent.

Opposite page:
Deer bound gracefully—and speedily—on spring-like legs. When leaping, a White-tailed Deer's front legs touch down at the same time.

Deer find it very tiring to trudge through snow looking for food. So in winter in northern areas, groups of deer gather together in one place that provides food and shelter from the wind. This activity is called *yarding*. The presence of many deer means that the snow gets tramped down and the animals can move around more easily. If food within the yard runs out, the deer tramp down trails or runways that lead to feeding spots beyond.

Danger!

At one time the wolf and the cougar were the deer's main *predators,* animals that hunt other animals for food. Today there are fewer of these animals left in the deer's range, so they are not as great a threat as they once were.

Dogs are now near the top of the deer's enemy list. Dogs are a danger especially in winter, when deer have trouble running on ice and snow.

A deer's main defenses are its speed and its keen senses. Except in winter, a deer can usually outrun its enemies, and it is constantly alert for

any sound, smell, or movement that might spell trouble. A deer also watches for warnings that come from the behavior of other deer.

Deer Warnings

If you've ever walked through the woods and heard what sounded like a big snort, you might have come close to a deer and not even have known it. When a deer is startled or nervous, it blows through its nose, making a snorty, sneezy sound. This clears the deer's nose and helps it sniff the air better. The noise may alert other deer, and it can be so loud that it even frightens away an enemy.

When alarmed, a deer might also thump the ground with its two front feet, as though playing a drum. This, too, warns other deer that danger is close by.

And a White-tailed Deer in full flight flips up its tail, showing the white fur underneath. This white tail acts as a warning flag. When other deer spot the signal, they dash away, their white tails flashing, too.

*Opposite page:
Any nearby deer will be quick to spot another White-tailed Deer's flashing white tail and understand its message: Danger!*

A Baby Is Born

In the fall—usually mid-November—deer *mate,* or come together to produce young. By late spring, the doe is ready to give birth. She sometimes picks a quiet spot in the shrubs as a nursery, but often her babies are born by the edge of a field where she has been nibbling grass.

A doe usually has one or two babies, called *fawns.* Sometimes three babies are born.

A newborn fawn weighs much the same as you did when you were born—6-7 pounds (about 3 kilograms). But within an hour of its birth, a fawn, unlike a human baby, can stand up by itself and even take a few wobbly steps on its long, spindly legs.

Even so, a fawn is still weak and helpless. Its mother leads it to a safe spot in shrubs or tall grass where it will be well hidden from predators. If a doe has two fawns, she hides each one in a different place.

A fawn's first steps may be wobbly, but it still performs an amazing feat: it can stand up by itself less than an hour after being born!

Built-in Protection

The fawn has a reddish-brown coat like its mother's—except for one important difference. The fawn's back is speckled with white spots—about 300 of them—each about the size of a quarter. These spots help protect the fawn from predators. When the fawn lies quietly in the bushes with its legs folded under its body and its chin flat on the ground, its enemies see only what looks like splashes of sunlight on the ground. Even a sharp-eyed eagle soaring overhead will be fooled by the fawn's spots and fly right by.

Besides not being able to see the fawn, predators will not be able to smell it either. For almost a week after it is born, a fawn does not give off any scent. The doe helps get rid of any tell-tale smell by giving the fawn a head-to-toe bath with her rough tongue as soon as it is born. She is so earnest in her cleaning that sometimes she may lick the fawn hard enough to knock it off its feet!

Lying perfectly still, its speckled coat blending into the pattern of light and shadow around it, this young fawn is quite well hidden from predators.

A Good Mother

A doe raises her family alone. The buck plays no part in looking after the young.

Once the doe hides her baby, she goes off to feed or rest nearby. She doesn't stay right beside her fawn because her presence might attract predators. But she does stay close enough to sniff the air for any scent of danger and to listen for any bleats from her little family.

Sometimes when people find a fawn alone in the woods they think it's an orphan or that it has been abandoned by its mother. That isn't true. The mother is close by even though people cannot see her.

Fawns drink milk from their mothers. A doe's milk is so rich that a fawn grows to nearly its mother's size in only four months.

40

First Outings

By the time the fawn is three weeks old, it has doubled its birth weight and is strong enough to follow its mother on her daily outings. At this age, a fawn is fast enough to outrun the average adult man!

It's easy for a fawn to wander away from its mother on these outings. But a doe will be able to find her fawn simply by using her nose. A deer has special glands in its hoofs that leave behind a scent trail when it walks. A mother doe will recognize her own fawn's scent and follow it to her lost baby.

Even though the fawn is still *nursing,* or drinking its mother's milk, it soon begins to nibble grass, dandelions, and tender leaves. Sometimes it even eats some of the leaves sticking out of the corners of its mother's mouth! When the time comes to take a first sip of water, a fawn might test-dip its nose in the pond several times before it finally takes a drink. Before long, it will be drinking about two quarts (nearly 2 liters) of water each day.

Opposite page: *A fawn practices leaping and bounding as it follows its mother on daily outings.*

Frisky Fawns

With all this eating and drinking, the fawn grows quickly. By the time it is two months old, it weighs as much as a four-year-old child. And in just another two months, it will be nearly as big as its mother! By then the fawn will have stopped nursing and will be losing its white spots as its winter coat begins to grow.

Fawns enjoy playing. They bound after their mother and chase grasshoppers and butterflies. Sometimes two fawns play a deer's version of leapfrog and jump over one another in turn. If there is a pond nearby, a fawn might hop in and splash up and down on all fours in the shallow water.

Under their mother's watchful eye, two young fawns stop to nibble on a snack of juicy grasses.

Growing Up

All this frisking and frolicking is fun, but it's more than just play. The fawns are developing strength, agility, and speed. And they are watching their mother and learning, from her example, to recognize signs of danger.

The fawns stay with their mother through their first winter. By spring, they're ready to take on the world by themselves. The young bucks will probably not mate for a year or two, until they are stronger and have grown bigger antlers. Most of the young does, however, will mate in the fall and will have their first babies the following spring.

Words To Know

Antlers   Hard, bony growths on the head of a male deer.

Blood vessels   Tubes, arteries, and veins through which blood flows in the body.

Buck   The male in many animal species, including the deer.

Cud   Hastily swallowed food brought up later for chewing by cud chewers such as cows and deer.

Den   Animal home or shelter.

Doe   The female in many animal species, including the deer.

Fawn   Baby deer.

Glade   An open space in a forest.

Hoofs   Feet of deer, cattle, and some other animals.

Mate   To come together to produce young.

Nurse   To drink milk from a mother's body.

Point   A spike or branch on a buck's antlers.

Predator   Animal that hunts other animals for food.

Swamp   Area where the ground stays wet and spongy most of the year.

Territory   Area that an animal or group of animals lives in and often defends from other animals of the same kind.

Velvet   Soft skin that covers a deer's antlers while they grow.

Yarding   The gathering together of deer for the winter in an area where food and shelter are available.

Index

Getting To Know...

Nature's Children

RABBITS

Merebeth Switzer

Grolier

Facts in Brief

Classification of North American rabbits and hares

Class: *Mammalia* (mammals)

Order: *Lagomorpha* ("hare-shaped" mammals)

Family: *Leporidae* (rabbit and hare family)

Genus: *Silvilagus* (rabbit); *Lepus* (hare)

Species: *Lepus americanus* (Snowshoe Hare); *Lepus arcticus* (Arctic Hare); several species of Cottontail and Jackrabbit

World distribution. Cottontails, Snowshoe and Arctic Hares, and Jackrabbits are native to North America. Other types of rabbits and hares are found worldwide with the exception of Antarctica and the islands of southeast Asia.

Distinctive physical characteristics. Cottontail: fluffy white tail. Arctic Hare: very large; relatively short ears and legs; white coat at least in winter, some all year. Snowshoe Hare: very large well-furred hind feet; coat changes color—brown in summer, white in winter. Jackrabbit: huge ears and very long legs.

Edited by: Elizabeth Grace Zuraw
Design/Photo Editor: Nancy Norton
Photo Rights: Ivy Images

ISBN: 0-7172-8490-5

Have you ever wondered . . .

We all know something about rabbits and hares, even if it's only from reading about the adventures of Bugs Bunny and Peter Rabbit, or watching their exploits on TV and videos.

We know that they all have big ears and short fluffy tails and that they hop. And most of them seem to get into trouble somewhere along the way by stealing garden vegetables.

You can probably think of many other storybook rabbits and hares. There's the March Hare in *Alice in Wonderland,* for instance, and that show-off who got taught a valuable lesson in Aesop's fable, *The Hare and the Tortoise.* And, of course, there's the Easter Bunny.

Certainly these storybook rabbits and hares are delightful and fascinating. But they're no more fascinating than the real rabbits and hares that roam our fields and woodlands. Let's find out more about these charming furry creatures.

Who wouldn't find this little Cottontail quite irresistible? Rabbits and their cousins, the hares, have long captured peoples' imaginations.

Rabbit
Length: 15-18 inches
(38-45 centimeters)
Weight: 1.5-4 pounds
(0.6-1.8 kilograms)

Hare
Length: 18-30 inches
(45-75 centimeters)
Weight: 4 pounds
(1.8 kilograms)

Rabbits or Hares: Who's Who?

Rabbits and hares are really quite different from each other, even though they look very much alike. It's often easy to confuse them—so easy, in fact, that some of them have been given the wrong names. The Jackrabbit, for example, is actually a hare, and the Belgian Hare is actually a rabbit!

So how do you tell them apart? Well, your best bet is to remember that rabbits generally are much smaller than hares and have shorter legs and ears. This, however, may not always be the case.

The only sure way to tell rabbits from hares is to get a look at them when they're newborn. Baby hares are born with open eyes and a full coat of fur, and they can hop a few hours after birth. Baby rabbits are born blind, helpless, and furless. It will be about a week before their eyes open, and nearly another week before they grow fur and can hop around.

Some rabbits and hares may be hard to tell apart, but there's no mistaking a Snowshoe Hare. Each huge, furry hind foot is more than one quarter the length of its body!

Rabbits, Rabbits Everywhere

Rabbits and hares are found all over the world except in Antarctica and the islands of southeast Asia. In some countries, such as Australia, there were no rabbits until fairly recent times. Early settlers brought some with them, and the animals quickly spread across the land.

In North America, rabbits and hares live in every type of wild area. Hares can live on the cold open tundra of the Arctic, in the hot desert, and high up in the Rocky Mountains. You can find rabbits in fields, swamps, marshes, and woods, and even in the parks of big cities. If you live in the country or in a small town, you may very well have seen a rabbit or two in your own yard or garden.

In North America, all rabbits are Cottontails, but there are several types of hares. The best

Where Cottontails are found in North America

Mother and baby Arctic Hare feast on the many kinds of plants that spring to life on the tundra during the short Arctic summer.

known are the Arctic Hare; the Snowshoe, or Varying, Hare; and the Jackrabbit.

Home Is Where You Find It

The hare does not have what we think of as a home. It simply uses whatever hiding place is available. This may be a clump of grass, a hollow log, or the low, overhanging branches of a fir tree. The hare will rest there all day with its body snuggled into the ground. This makes a shallow hollow called a *form*. A hare may use several forms, but it will usually have a favorite one that is "home."

In the winter, some hares may tunnel a short way into the snow and scratch out a cozy nook for a shelter.

In winter, home to a Snowshoe Hare is often a low-hanging evergreen branch that shelters it from wind and falling snow.

Just as people around the world are different from each other, so are rabbits and hares. In Europe, rabbits make *burrows,* holes dug in the earth, and live in *warrens,* underground communities that consist of many burrows in the same area. North American rabbits, on the other hand, follow the hare's example and use forms for sleeping. No one knows why North American rabbits do not dig burrows. It's not that they dislike them, because they do occasionally borrow someone else's—usually a woodchuck's or a skunk's.

Like many "rules" in nature, however, this one has an exception. One kind of Cottontail, the tiny Pygmy Rabbit that lives in the southwestern United States, does dig its own burrow.

A nook in a snowbank might not suit everyone, but it really can be quite comfortable—if you're a hare.

Getting Along with Each Other

Rabbits, Jackrabbits, and Snowshoe Hares usually live alone. Jackrabbits, in fact, seldom mix at all, even with their own kind. The others, however, are quite friendly with their close relatives and are sometimes seen feeding together or playing tag on a moonlit field.

On the other hand, the northern Snowshoe Hares and Arctic Hares are often found in large groups of more than 100 animals. In these groups, aunts, uncles, brothers, and sisters share the same feeding grounds and often play together in mock battles and chasing games.

Although rabbits and hares are friendly toward their own kind, they are not friendly toward each other. You'll rarely find rabbits and hares together in the wild.

It's easy to see how an Artic Hare's white fur protects it from enemies. These hares blend so well with their snowy surroundings that they can barely be seen.

Dinnertime

Rabbits and hares are most active at night. They spend the day in their forms, snoozing and *grooming*—cleaning themselves by licking their fur. Then when it begins to get dark, they come out to look for food. It's safer for them to move around when they can't be seen.

Rabbits and hares are *herbivores,* animals that eat mainly plants. There's nothing a rabbit likes better than fresh greens, and it doesn't care where it finds them. No wonder farmers and gardeners sometimes think they're pests!

Rabbits and hares are active all year, always searching for food. During the northern winter, they feed on twigs, buds, and the bark of certain trees. In the Arctic, where everything is covered with snow most of the time, hares dig down to get buried moss and *lichen* (which is pronounced *LIKE-en),* flowerless plants that grow on rocks and trees. Arctic Hares need up to a pound (0.5 kilograms) of food per day. Sometimes, in order to survive the Arctic winter, they will eat meat if they find it.

Opposite page:
This Cottontail nibbles on a favorite snack—tender young sprouts.

Better Than a Knife and Fork

Rabbits and hares have a set of special front teeth to help them snip off plants and twigs for their dinner. Kangaroos can hop, and elephants have big ears—and hares and rabbits have big ears and can hop, too— but no other animal has teeth quite like those of our little furry friends.

Other animals—squirrels, for instance— have two big front upper teeth for cutting, just as rabbits and hares do. But rabbits and hares have an extra pair of smaller, very sharp front teeth just behind the big ones. This extra pair of cutting teeth is one of the main features that makes rabbits and hares different from all other animals.

Like all rabbits and hares, this Desert Cottontail has special front teeth to snip off greens for its meals.

The powerful back legs of rabbits and especially hares enable them to jump high and fast. This European Hare can make gigantic leaps, even from a standing start.

Getting Around

You probably know that rabbits and hares don't walk. They hop. But do you know what truly champion hoppers they are? If a Snowshoe Hare were as big as you, it would win all the gold medals in high jumping and broad jumping. In one hop, a Snowshoe Hare can jump 15 feet (4.5 meters) straight up and can cover a distance about ten times its own length!

And they're fast, too. Hares have been recorded moving at nearly 50 miles (80 kilometers) per hour over short distances! That's the speed at which many cars travel. Rabbits are a bit slower. They can reach less than about half that speed.

Showshoe Hare's hind foot

How rabbits and hares hop.

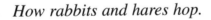

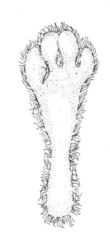

Jackrabbit's hind foot

How can a rabbit or hare jump that far, that high, and that fast? The secret is in its powerful back legs—they're huge and full of muscles. No wonder the hare in Aesop's fable didn't worry about the tortoise in their race!

There is one type of rabbit that not only hops, it swims and even dives underwater. It's the Marsh, or Swamp, Rabbit, a type of Cottontail found in the southeastern United States.

To keep cool on hot summer days, these rabbits are even seen lolling about in ponds or puddles!

Although they move fast, rabbits and hares seldom go very far. Most, in fact, spend their entire lives within 1,300 feet (400 meters) of their homes. The Jackrabbit may roam twice as far, however, and if food is scarce, all will venture beyond their usual *range,* or feeding grounds. During mating season as well, males may go courting outside their home range.

Snowshoe Hare tracks in snow

Marsh—or Swamp—Rabbits, like the one shown here, get their name because they like living in wet, swampy areas.

Starting a Family

Baby rabbits and hares are born in the spring and summer, when the weather is warm enough for them to survive.

When the first signs of spring appear, adult rabbits and hares begin their *mating season,* the time when they come together to produce young. The males, called *bucks,* fight each other to decide who will father the young, while the female, the *doe,* waits nearby. Once the fight is settled, there may be an elaborate *courting dance,* a dance performed by male and female animals during mating time. The buck chases the doe and flags his tail. The two then dance around each other, play-box, and leap high into the air. Sometimes they groom each other by licking the other's fur and nuzzling.

Born in spring and summer, rabbits and hares grow fast. By the age of six months, this Cottontail will be a full-grown adult, ready to start its own family.

Rabbit Families

In southern Canada and the northern United States, a mother rabbit may have three to five separate *litters,* or families, between March and September. In warmer climates she may have even more.

About four weeks after mating, the doe gets ready for the birth. She makes a nest in a shallow hole in the ground and carefully lines it with soft grasses and plants. She adds pieces of fur plucked from her own coat to make the nest extra warm for her babies. The nest is small and will have room enough for only the young babies, called *kits.*

Each time a doe gives birth, she has a litter of five or six babies. The kits are tiny—only about 3 inches (8 centimeters) long. They cannot see and are completely helpless. Shortly after the birth, the mother allows her babies to *nurse,* to drink milk from her body.

These baby rabbits are probably about a week old. Their eyes are open, their furry coat is growing, and in a few days they'll be up on their feet.

Then, to protect her babies, she covers the nest with pieces of plants before she moves a distance away.

Keeping the Babies Safe

During the first two weeks, the doe leaves the kits alone except when it's time for them to nurse. Even then, she approaches the nest in a zigzag pattern, leaping the last few feet in order not to leave a trail. In this way she keeps the babies' hiding place a secret from *predators,* animals that hunt other animals for food.

In their nest, the kits are safe from most wild animals. But their open nursery can sometimes place them in danger at the hands of well-meaning people. A person who finds a nest often thinks that the mother has abandoned her babies. Not so! The mother is very near, and is looking after her family in the best possible way. Baby rabbits are difficult to care for, and have a far better chance of surviving if people leave them alone.

Opposite page:
A rabbit nest is small, having just enough room for the kits. But it's quite comfortable, thank you, with sisters and brothers making nice soft pillows for each other.

Hare Families

Hares usually have fewer litters than rabbits do, and the litters are smaller in size. The mother hare behaves differently from the mother rabbit. She does not make a nest but simply stops at the nearest sheltered spot when she is ready to give birth. The chipmunk-sized babies, called *leverets,* are born covered with warm fur. Although they can see and are able to hop around a few hours after birth, the leverets still need their mother's care.

Sleeping is what baby Arctic Hares—like human babies—do best.

The mother hare nurses her babies once a day under cover of darkness. This is her way of keeping their hiding spot safe from predators. Like a mother rabbit, she leaves her babies alone the rest of the time but remains nearby, ready to chase enemies away. While their mother is gone, the babies huddle together in a warm brown heap for protection. Luckily they can soon scamper away to hide if any danger comes near.

Both kits and leverets grow very quickly. Leverets are ready to leave the nest at three weeks, and the kits, which have more growing up to do, leave home at five or six weeks. Brothers and sisters may stay together for a few weeks before going their separate ways.

A baby Snowshoe Hare blends in so well with its surroundings that it's hard to tell where baby stops and surroundings begin!.

Jackrabbits

Jackrabbits are actually very long-legged, long-eared hares. There are three main types of Jackrabbit: the Black-tailed Jackrabbit, the White-tailed Jackrabbit, and the giant-eared Antelope Jackrabbit. You can guess how the first two got their names, but what about the third? The Antelope Jackrabbit is named for its white rump, which looks like the rump of the Pronghorn, or American Antelope.

The Jackrabbit's huge ears are super scopes for picking up sound, but they also serve another purpose: they help keep the hare's body cool in summer. The hare's blood flows into its ears and is cooled by breezes blowing across them. This helps to cool the whole body.

Where Jackrabbits are found in North America

Like all Jackrabbits, the one shown here has a built-in air-conditioning system: its ears!

The Snowshoe Hare

This hare lives in the forest. The name *snowshoe* refers to its very large hind feet. These act like built-in snowshoes and help the hare move over deep snow without sinking up to its furry nose. They're even better than regular snowshoes because they are covered with thick, bristly fur that helps keep the four big toes on each foot warm.

The Snowshoe, or Varying, Hare has a long, thick white coat in the winter to keep it warm and serve as a disguise. In the spring it sheds this coat and grows a brown summer coat. The new hair is shorter and thinner and helps the hare hide among the shadows of the forest.

Snowshoe Hares often create year-round trails or runways through heavy brush. The runways go between favorite feeding and resting spots, and they are often used by squirrels, porcupines, skunks, and other animals.

Where Snowshoe Hares are found in North America

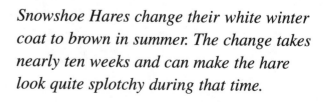

Snowshoe Hares change their white winter coat to brown in summer. The change takes nearly ten weeks and can make the hare look quite splotchy during that time.

The Arctic Hare

The Arctic Hare is like the Snowshoe Hare, but it's nearly three times bigger. A large body is needed in the icy North. It keeps warmer than a small body and takes longer to cool down. This hare also has unusually short ears and legs. The shorter ears and legs are closer to the hare's body and help to keep it warmer. They do not allow the body to cool the way the long legs and ears of Jackrabbits do.

The Arctic Hare has a special fur coat made of two layers. Long silky fur lies over a layer of shorter woolly fur next to the body. The top layer keeps out the wind, and the bottom layer supplies warmth.

To save energy, the Arctic Hare spends much of its time sitting very still, looking like a statue. It tucks its tail and paws under its

Where Arctic Hares are found in North America

That's some winter coat! Two thick layers of special fur warm up and puff out this cozy Arctic Hare.

body and flattens its ears along its back. It sits this way sheltered behind rocks and snowdrifts or out in the open, facing into the wind. The wind presses the fur tightly against the hare's body, which helps keep in the heat.

In the southern part of their range, Arctic Hares grow a new brownish coat for summer. In the northern Arctic, however, summer is only a few weeks long. Hares living there don't change their white coats. This makes them very visible in summer against the brown tundra.

The short summer in the part of the world where the Arctic Hare lives allows for the birth of only one litter of three to six babies each year. The leverets are grayish-brown at birth, which allows them to blend into their summer surroundings.

White coats make these northern Arctic Hares easy to spot against the brown summer tundra.

A Dangerous Life

Rabbits and most hares have many babies each year. In two years, a normal rabbit's lifespan, two pairs of rabbits could produce more than 160 children and 3,000 grandchildren. Now, that's a lot of rabbits!

If all the rabbits and hares survived, we'd be knee-deep in bunnies. Why doesn't this happen? Because small animals such as rabbits are very important to the balance of nature. They are dinner for foxes, owls, coyotes, weasels, lynx, and many other animals.

With so many predators looking for a meal, rabbits and hares must use all their wits to survive. They are always alert to danger, even when they take a short nap. Their huge ears catch every sound, and their constantly twitching nose sniffs the air for intruders. Through the ground they feel the vibrations caused by people or other animals passing by.

A hare's huge hind feet provide a good support when the animal dashes to escape enemies.

Survival Tricks

If an intruder moves near, rabbits and hares flatten their ears and crouch close to the ground. If the danger comes nearer still, they flatten their body even further. In this position they look like a small rock, and may fool an enemy.

When it appears that there is no escape from discovery, the rabbit or hare explodes from its crouch, leaping 6-15 feet (2-4.5 meters) from a standing start. It then streaks away, hopping this way and that in a tricky zigzag pattern. This movement makes it very difficult for predators to follow.

Although rabbits and hares are usually silent creatures, all of them are capable of letting out a terrible, ear-piercing scream when they are captured or in serious danger. This tremendous shriek may result in their being dropped quickly by their startled attacker.

Rabbits and hares have a special ability to hop, jump, leap, and zigzag every which way as they streak forward. These lightning-fast movements enable the animals to make fast getaways.

A New Bunny Season

Young rabbits and hares newly out on their own are in particular danger. They haven't yet learned all their parents' survival tricks. Many unwary youngsters fall prey to a watchful owl, fox, or other predator.

The rabbit or hare that survives these first difficult weeks will soon be ready to start its own family. With luck, a rabbit will live to one or two years of age. Hares may live for three or more years.

Words To Know

Buck   The male in many animal species, including the rabbit and hare.

Burrow   A hole dug in the ground by an animal for use as a home.

Courting dance   A dance, always following the same pattern, that is performed by male and female animals during the mating season.

Desert   Hot, dry area with few plants or trees.

Doe   The female in many animal species, including the rabbit and hare.

Form   A hollow in the ground made by a rabbit or hare to be used as a home or resting place.

Grooming   Brushing or cleaning hair or fur.

Herbivore   Animal that eats mainly plants.

Kit   Baby rabbit.

Leveret   Baby hare.

Lichen   A flowerless, moss-like plant that grows on rocks and trees.

Litter   Group of animal brothers and sisters born together.

Marsh   Soft, wet land.

Mate   To come together to produce young.

Mating season   The time of year during which animals mate.

Nurse   To drink milk from a mother's body.

Predator   An animal that hunts other animals for food.

Range   The area in which an animal feeds and lives.

Swamp   Area where the ground stays wet and spongy most of the year.

Tundra   Flat land in the Arctic where no trees grow.

Warren   Piece of ground containing many rabbit burrows.

Index

PHOTO CREDITS
Cover: William Lowry. **Interiors:** *Valan Photos:* Wayne Lankinen, 4; Stephen J. Krasemann, 7, 16, 32, 35, 37, 41; Brian Milne, 8, 30; François Morneau, 11; Albert Kuhnigk, 12; Kennon Cooke, 19; Esther Schmidt, 24; Harold V. Green, 27, 28, 43. /David R. Gray, 15, 39. /Bill Ivy, 20. /Hot Shots: J. D. Taylor, 23, 45.